SMART BRAIN RIGHT BRAIN

The Natural World Around Us

Om KIDZ
An imprint of Om Books International

First Published in 2021 by

Om Kidz | Om Books International

Corporate & Editorial Office
A-12, Sector 64, Noida 201 301
Uttar Pradesh, India
Phone: +91 120 477 4100
Email: editorial@ombooks.com
Website: www.ombooksinternational.com

Sales Office
107, Ansari Road, Darya Ganj
New Delhi 110 002, India
Phone: +91 11 4000 9000
Email: sales@ombooks.com

Author: Shweta Sinha
Editor: Kirti Pathak
Art & Design: Anshuman Pandey, Gaurav Bhandari, Harish Arya

ISBN: 978-93-5276-831-8

Printed in India

10 9 8 7 6 5 4 3 2 1

CONTENTS

1. The World Around Us

Imagine a world with no animals or plants in it. Not only are there no dogs or cats, but also no lions, tigers, dolphins or bears. And no jungles with monkeys and deer either. No colourful flowers, no fruits nor trees to provide shade. How boring such a world would be!

The natural world

It is easy to think that everything around us is made entirely by human beings. The houses we live in, the cars we ride, the roads we walk on—are all built by us. But the fact is that we cannot survive without the natural world.

The natural world forms our environment. It includes all the animals, plants and other things that exist in nature and share the planet with us.

We depend on plants and animals for our food and air. We need fresh air to breathe and food to give us energy. Plants and animals provide us these necessities.

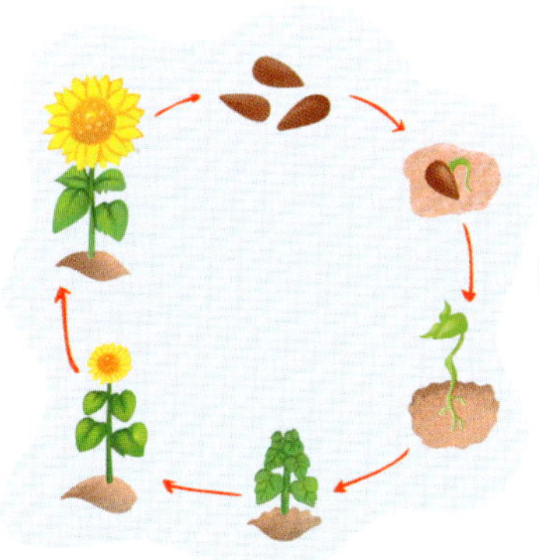

POCKET FACT

Plants have existed for around 400 million years. Humans have been around only for about 200,000 years.

Living vs. non-living

Look at this doggy below. It looks just like the real one on the right. But it is not. It is just a toy made of cloth and plastic. You don't need to feed it or walk it. This toy is a non-living thing.

Our world is full of living and non-living things.
What makes the toy (non-living thing) different from a real dog (living thing)?

- Living things breathe.
- Living things eat.
- Living things move and grow.
- Living things make babies.

DID YOU KNOW?

Coal and wood are non-living things that once had life. Both come from plants.

2. The Food We Eat

The food we eat gives us energy to work, walk, run, jump or perform any other activity.

Where do we get our food from?

Humans get their food from plants and animals.

Food that we get from plants:

- Fruits and Vegetables
- Cooking Oil
- Spices
- Sugar

What else can you think of?

Food that we get from animals:

- Meat
- Milk
- Eggs

POCKET FACT

We grow 2,000 different types of plants across the world for the various kinds of food humans eat.

Sources of food

Like humans, animals too depend on plants or other animals for food. Plants, on the other hand, make their own food. Plants need water, soil and sunlight to survive. Their leaves produce food through a process called **Photosynthesis**.

Hence, plants are called **'Producers'**.

Since animals and humans depend on others for food, they are known as '**Consumers**'.

Do you think all animals eat the same kind of food?

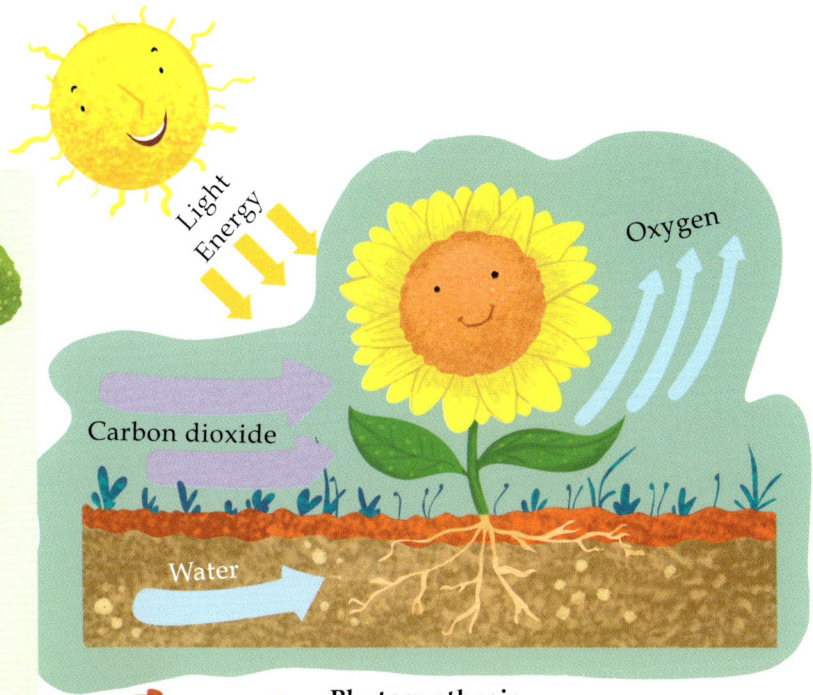

Photosynthesis

DID YOU KNOW?

We eat almost every part of plants. The carrot is a root, potato is a stem while broccoli is a flower.

3. Who Eats What?

Different animals eat different food. Animals like deer and rabbit eat food from plants directly. Animals that eat mainly plants are known as **herbivores**.

The cow, giraffe, zebra, horse, squirrel are all herbivores.

Then there are animals, like the lion, that eat only meat. They prey on other animals and consume their flesh. Such animals are called **carnivores**.

The wolf, tiger, cheetah, fox, shark are carnivores.

There are also animals that eat both plants and animals. They are called **omnivores**.

The bear, dog, cat, monkey, seagull are **omnivores**.

POCKET FACT

Human beings can eat both plants and animals. They are omnivorous.

Food chain

These different food habits form an interesting chain. Herbivores consume plants. Herbivores are in turn consumed by carnivores or omnivores.

In this chain, **producers** or plants create energy from the sun. This energy is transferred to animals that eat the plants. And then it gets transferred to other animals that eat those animals.

Hence, herbivores or plant eaters are '**primary consumers**' as they get their nutrition directly from plants.

An animal that gets its nutrition by consuming another animal is called a '**secondary consumer**'.

DID YOU KNOW?

If there were no sun, plants would not produce energy. If plants stopped producing, none of us would survive.

4. The Web of Life

Animals, plants and humans depend on each other for their food requirements. An easy way to show this dependence is as a picture:

DID YOU KNOW?

Although humans are omnivores, many people choose not to eat meat and fish. They are called vegetarians.

The plant is a producer. It makes its own food from the sun.

The caterpillar is a primary consumer. It feeds on the flowers and leaves of the plants.

The caterpillar is eaten by the frog, which gets eaten by the snake.

The owl eats the snake.

This inter-dependence of living-things where one eats the other to survive is called the **Food Chain**.

Food web

In nature, many food chains are linked together. This forms a **food web**.

Look at this diagram. How many primary consumers can you see here?

Here, the sparrow is both a primary consumer as well as a carnivore. As a carnivore, it feeds on both caterpillar and snail. So, the sparrow is a part of more than one food chains.

Similarly, the caterpillar is eaten by both the chameleon and the sparrow and is a part of more than one food chain too.

Follow the arrows to identify all the food chains in this food web.

POCKET FACT

When an animal dies, decomposers (fungi and bacteria) break down the dead animal into nutrients for the soil. Plants consume those nutrients to grow.

What happens if an organism in the food chain gets affected or disappears?

Ripple effect

A lot of the chemicals we use at home, in factories and the fertilisers from farms, find their way into rivers. The river receives so much toxic material that it is unable to wash it away. These chemicals kill aquatic life directly. They also promote the growth of algae. Algae are tiny bright green plants that grow so rapidly that other plants do not survive around them. Algae also suck oxygen out of the water, smothering the fish.

With less plants to feed on, the insect population decreases. Fishes that eat the insects begin dying as well, due to low food supply. As the fish population dwindles, it means less food for the people who depend on the fish. When a species disappears, it affects one or more species in the food chain. Hence, all animals and plants, even the tiniest of insects, are important in the natural world.

More prey, less predators

Extinction of a species higher up in the food chain has a ripple effect downwards too. In central and eastern U.S, the population of deer saw a great increase. This was because their predators-the wolves and cougars- were reducing in numbers. More deer in the same area ate more plants, trees and grass. This changed the green cover of the region and resulted in a reduced forest area.

DID YOU KNOW?

Extremely small pieces of plastic have been found in the bellies of some fishes. This came from the plastic trash we dump into the oceans.

5. Where Is My Home?

Why don't coconut trees grow on mountains? Or Polar bears live in deserts?

Coconut trees grow best in warm coastal areas by the sea. They need sandy, brackish soil to grow, lots of rainfall and abundant sunlight. The sea disperses their fruit so more coconut trees can grow from them. On a mountain, the coconut tree would not get regular rainfall or enough sunlight. It will also be unable to survive the extreme cold winters.

DID YOU KNOW?

A greenhouse is a building that lets you grow plants in controlled climatic conditions. That's how you can grow a tropical plant in a cold region.

Polar bears live on top of the ice that covers the Arctic sea. This is where they hunt, live, breed and rear their young cubs. They need lots of meat and fat to eat. The sea ice lets them easily hunt for seals, their main food. The snow lets them hide from predators and prey. A desert would be too hot for the polar bear. It also would not have enough prey to feed its huge body. So we see that every plant and animal needs the right environment to survive.

POCKET FACT

A polar bear's skin is black underneath the fur, the best colour for absorbing heat from the sun.

What is a habitat?

All living things live in an environment that provides them with everything they need to survive, such as food and shelter. The environment where a living thing normally lives and grows is called its **habitat**.

POCKET FACT

Different species of animals and plants living in a habitat depend on each other. Together they create a balanced web of life called an ecosystem.

Different habitats of the world

Our Earth has a variety of geographical features and weather conditions. The environment differs greatly from place to place. Some areas have mountains, while others are covered with water. Some regions receive snowfall, others remain burning hot and dry throughout the year. How many different habitats can you think of?

Aquatic

Aqua stands for water. All habitats in water are called '**Aquatic**'.

Seas and oceans have salty water. They are the largest habitats in the world. You can find huge marine animals like whales and sharks living there. Starfish and seaweed are other common residents here.

Rivers, lakes and ponds have freshwater. Fish, frog, duck, water lily and cattail are commonly found in freshwater habitats.

Coastal habitats lie where the land meets the sea. Coconut trees grow well in coastal areas.

Mountains and polar regions

Mountains and polar habitats are the coldest in the world. They have lots of snow and ice. Trees here are cone-shaped with needle-like leaves. Animals have adapted themselves to withstand the harsh climate. They have fat layers to protect them from the cold weather. Some have thick fur or feathers too. Apart from polar bears, you can find penguins, snow leopards, seals and walruses.

Deserts

A desert is an area with scarce rainfall. In hot deserts, temperatures can reach as high as 50 degree Celsius. Only animals and plants that survive the hot, dry conditions live and grow here. The cactus has a fleshy stem to store water. Aloe Vera is a plant native to North Africa and looks like a cactus. It has fleshy leaves instead of a fleshy stem. The camel stores fat in its hump to survive days without food and water. The scorpion and desert fox, among others, live in deserts.

POCKET FACT

Both cactus and aloe vera have prickles to prevent animals from eating them for water.

Grasslands

Grasslands are vast areas with tall grass and colourful, wild flowers. Rainfall is not enough to grow many trees. The abundance of grass attracts lots of grazing animals. Grasslands located close to the equator (middle of the Earth) are hot all the time. Those away from the equator have hot summers and cold winters.

Savannah- African grasslands that receive rainfall in one season only. The baobab tree has a huge swollen trunk to store water, allowing it to survive months of drought. Zebras, giraffes and elephants are hunted here by lions and hyenas.

Prairie- Grasslands in North America where the mighty bisons roam and the prairie dogs hunt.

Steppe- Here trees grow only near lakes and rivers. Steppes are located across Europe, Asia and the Americas.

Veld- Grasslands in southern Africa. Go here to see the cheetahs, lions and antelopes.

Baobabs in Savannah

Wild flowers and grass in the Prairie

Steppe in Mongolia

Veld of Southern Africa

DID YOU KNOW?

The narrow leaves of grass reduce water loss and make the plant drought-resistant.

Forests

Forests are large areas full of trees and plants. Almost half of our Earth is covered with forests. There are three types of forests:

1. **Rainforests** lie close to the equator and are jam-packed with tall trees. The climate is warm with abundant rain. More than half of the world's plant and animal species are found here. Orchids, ferns and moss are common in rainforests and so are monkeys, bats and a variety of insects.

2. **Temperate** forests have warm summers and cold winters. Foxes, eagles, squirrels and bears live around maple, oak and elm trees.

3. **Boreal** or Taiga forests grow in areas close to the North Pole. Temperatures range from a freezing -50° C to a warm 30° C. Trees, like the pine and the fir are evergreen and cone-shaped to prevent snow from piling on their branches. Animals include snow rabbits, wolves, foxes, deer, and chipmunks.

DID YOU KNOW? The popular comic character 'Tarzan' lived in a rainforest with his gorilla family and swung on vines that grew around the tall trees.

6. Adapting to Habitats

All animals and plants have their own favourite habitat. They are well-adapted to survive in their natural surroundings.

Structural adaptation

Like other desert animals, the camel hardly sweats to prevent loss of water. Their padded hooves help them walk on sand and long eyelashes protect their eyes during a sandstorm. A desert fox has short fur to stay cool and large ears to lose heat.

A panda has thick fur to stay warm in the mountains and small ears to stop heat-loss. A snow rabbit's fur turns white in winters and brown in summers for camouflage.

Fish have streamlined bodies and fins to swim easily. Birds have pointed bills to help pick up worms from holes in trees.

Behavioural adaptation

Animals adapt by making changes in the way they live.

- Bears hibernate or sleep for long periods to survive the cold winter months.
- Grasslands are dry and prone to fire that spreads quickly. Animals in grasslands can run very fast to escape wildfires.
- Most desert animals live inside burrows and venture out at night to avoid the heat.
- Squirrels gather and store food to consume during winter months when food is scarce.

DID YOU KNOW?

A King snake looks like the dangerous coral snake to scare off predators. Eels are fishes that resemble snakes. They are sometimes called fake snakes.

- Some animals migrate short distances to find food or for a safer place to live and breed. Siberian Cranes fly out from the Tundra in Russia to China and Iran to escape the harsh winters.

Adaptation vs. acclimatisation

Adaptation is any change in an organism that takes place over a long period of time. However, sometimes organisms change over a short period of time to adjust to a change in its surroundings. A chameleon changes its colour for camouflage to escape being spotted by other animals. This is called **acclimatisation**.

DID YOU KNOW?

Little brown bats have a unique adaptation to survive different weather conditions. They spend their summer hanging from trees but move to sheltered caves during cold weather.

7. The Human Factor

Most of us love animals, but a lot of things that we do end up harming them. The way we live affects everything around us, including animals and plants.

Habitat destruction is one the main reasons that threaten animals today. Imagine if your home gets destroyed and you have nowhere to go. That is how animals feel when their homes get destroyed. The Asian elephants once used to dominate the low-growing forests from Iraq to China. But increasing human population saw forests being cut down to build cities and towns. We were taking over the elephants' homes and destroying their habitat. In the last 50 years, the elephant numbers went down by half!

Large areas in the Amazon rainforest in Brazil have been taken over by farms and ranches. Mining projects in Mongolia threaten the snow leopard's habitat in the mountains.

Climate Change is another big threat to habitats worldwide. Arctic ice has been fast melting away because of rising global temperatures. Polar bears live on the sea ice and depend on it to reach their prey, the seals. Without their habitat, they risk starving to death. Rising temperatures also caused the bush fires in Australia that killed thousands of animals. We contribute to this global warming by burning more and more fossil fuels—in cars, factories, electricity production, and more. Cutting down forests means lesser trees to reverse the effects of global warming.

Pollution damages habitats and kills animals. Pollution is when we add things to our environment that contaminates it or makes it dirty. We find rivers and streams full of chemicals from factories and homes. Trash is piling up in landfills. The air is filled with smoke.

All this poisons the air, water and soil, affecting the ecosystem. Plastic is one of the most widely used materials. It is everywhere around us. Do you know that plastic stays in the environment for up to 500 years? Plastic does not decompose; it only breaks down into smaller and smaller pieces. Animals eat this plastic, mistaking it for food. Sea turtles have often ingested plastic waste that have caused blockages in their stomachs. Little birds have entangled themselves and died in plastic nets.

Overhunting and **overfishing** have led to the extinction of a great many species. Many animals disappeared from Earth only because humans hunted them until none was left. Rhinos get killed for their horn, even though it is illegal to hunt them. Humans have been taking out more fish out of the seas than the fishes can reproduce. This has pushed some species to the brink of extinction.

DID YOU KNOW?

Every twenty-four hours, 150-200 species of plant or animal life goes extinct due to climate change.

8. Saving the Planet

We can all adopt ways by which we can protect the Earth and its inhabitants.

Reduce, Reuse, Recycle

Limit your use of plastic. Carry your own shopping bag. Use a reusable bottle for water instead of buying bottled water. Avoid disposable cutlery. Recycle glass bottles and aluminium cans. Stop wasting paper. Save water and conserve energy.

Take care of wildlife

Light pollution harms creatures like the fireflies. Avoid using bright lights outdoors. Don't capture butterflies and moths. It harms their wings. Bugs are important to the environment too. Don't trample on them. Don't keep exotic animals as pets. These animals thrive in their natural habitat only. Plant a sapling every year on your birthday and take good care of it.

POCKET FACT

The World Environment day is celebrated on 5th June every year.

9. Let's Make Seed Bombs

Make seed bombs and grow plants wherever you want to.

You need:

- Flower seeds
- Compost
- Water
- Mixing bowl
- Clay soil or powdered clay

1. In a bowl, mix together 1 cup of seeds with 5 cups of compost and 2-3 cups of clay soil. Blend all three well with your hands.	
2. Slowly pour water and keep mixing until everything sticks together. The mixture should be soft and sticky like play dough. Make sure not to pour water too quickly, else you may end up adding too much.	
3. Take small portions of the clay mix and roll it into balls.	
4. Leave the balls to dry out in the sun.	

Your seeds bombs are ready. Toss them into empty parts of your garden and see tiny saplings pop out in a few days.

Let's Get Active

Choose the correct answer:

1. A wolf is a
   (a) Prey (b) Primary Consumer
   (c) Carnivorous animal (d) Producer
2. A food chain starts with
   (a) Humans (b) Predators
   (c) Primary Consumers (d) Plants
3. Bears and humans are
   (a) Omnivores (b) Carnivores
   (c) Herbivores (d) Producers
4. Baobab trees grow in the
   (a) Veld (b) Prairie
   (c) Steppe (d) Savannah
5. Cactus and aloe vera have ______to protect themselves from animals
   (a) Bad smell (b) Prickles
   (c) Poison (d) Bad taste
6. Without ________polar bears might go extinct.
   (a) Snow (b) Trees
   (c) Arctic sea ice (d) Oceans
7. Bears _______during winters.
   (a) Hunt (b) Migrate
   (c) Gather food (d) Hibernate
8. The pine tree is ________ to stop snow from collecting on it
   (a) Cone-shaped (b) Spread out
   (c) Deep-rooted (d) Wide-bottomed

The Natural World

Circle everything in the picture below that does not belong to the Natural World:

Adaptation

Explain the adaptation in the living things below:

A desert fox lives in hot, dry places

....

....

A snow rabbit lives in boreal forests

....

....

A penguin lives in cold places

....

....

Grass that grows in hot grasslands

....

....

A place to stay

Where do these animals normally live? Draw a line to match the animals to their habitat:

Grasslands

Aquatic

Bison
Black bear
Crab
Crocodile
Dolphin
Elephant
Fox
Frog
Lion
Mountain goat
Rabbit
Red Panda
Shark
Snow leopard
Tiger
Wolf
Zebra

Forest

Mountains

GLOSSARY

Abundant	a lot of
Algae	a type of plant-like living thing
Brackish	saline; with high salt content
Camouflage	a way of hiding something so that it looks like its surroundings
Climate change	when there is a big difference in normal climate patterns over a long period of time
Consume	to eat or drink
Decomposers	they consume dead animals and plants and reduce them into simpler matter
Drought	a shortage of rain over a long period of time
Environment	all the physical surroundings on Earth
Equator	an imaginary line that divides the Earth into the northern and southern parts
Extinction	when every single member of a species dies out
Global warming	a slow and steady rise in Earth's surface temperature
Migrate	to move from one country or region to another
Nutrition	the study of food and how it works in your body
Photosynthesis	the process in which green plants use sunlight to make their own food
Pollution	things in the environment that contaminate it or make it dirty
Population	the number of organisms of the same species that live in a particular area at the same time
Predator	an animal that kills another animal for food

ANSWERS

Page 28. 1. (c) 2. (d) 3. (a) 4. (d) 5. (b) 6. (c) 7. (d) 8. (a)

Page 30. Desert Fox- Short fur to keep it cool; large ears to lose heat
Snow Rabbit- Its fur turns white in winters and brown in summers for camouflage
Penguin- Thick feathers and body fat to stay warm
Grass- deep roots to absorb water from the soil. Narrow leaves to prevent water-loss

Page 31. Grasslands- Bison, elephant, lion, zebra
Forest- Fox, rabbit, tiger, wolf
Aquatic- Crab, crocodile, dolphin, shark, frog
Mountains- Black bear, red panda, mountain goat, snow leopard